Library of Congress Cataloging-in-Publication Data Grand slam gifts. p. cm. ISBN 0-86573-989-7 1. Handicraft. 2. Sports in art. 3. Gifts. I. Cy DeCosse Incorporated.   TT157.G634 1996 745.5 — dc20 96-15852 CIP

Table of Contents

BALL *Display* stands

If you know someone who has an autographed basketball, caught a home-run ball at a baseball game, or saved a football from their high school championship team, give them a stand on which to display their prized possession.

You'll find instructions for making a simple but stylish ball stand on the following pages. The stand goes together quickly and requires few tools. Stain it to match home decor or paint it in the colors of a favorite team. Small brass plaques can be purchased and engraved at gift stores or trophy stores, then mounted on the base of the stand.

Ball display Stand

MATERIALS

❖Solid hardwood or medium-density fiberboard, ³/₄" (2 cm) thick ❖Jig saw or craft saw ❖100-grit sandpaper ❖Wood glue ❖Two C-clamps ❖Drill and ³/₈" drill bit ❖Masking tape ❖³/₈" (1 cm) wooden dowel ❖Stain or paint in desired color ❖Small, engraved brass plaque, optional

1 Measure wood for two boards to dimensions indicated below, opposite; mark with pencil. Cut boards from wood, using saw. Sand the edges smooth with sandpaper.

2 Center smaller board on top board; secure with wood glue. Clamp the boards together with C-clamps, using pieces of scrap wood between boards and clamps to protect boards. Wipe excess glue away with damp rag. Allow glue to dry.

3 Remove clamps. Mark a point on top board one square inch (2.5 square cm) in at each corner.

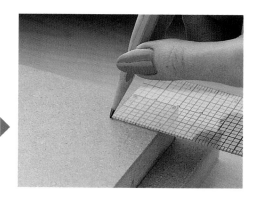

4 Wrap a piece of masking tape around drill bit with edge of tape 1" (2.5 cm) from tip of bit. Drill holes at each marked point on top board; stop drilling when edge of tape meets surface of wood. Sand edges of holes smooth with sandpaper.

5 Cut four pieces of dowel to length indicated below. Sand ends smooth with sandpaper. Place a drop of glue in each drilled hole; secure dowels in the holes. Wipe excess glue away with damp rag. Allow glue to dry.

6 Stain or paint ball stand as desired. Allow to dry. Secure brass plaque on stand.

Dimensions for Football Stand

- **Bottom board:** 6" × 8" (15 × 20.5 cm) rectangle

- **Top board:** 4½" × 6½" (11.5 × 16.3 cm) rectangle

- **Dowels:** 5" (12.5 cm) long

Dimensions for Softball or Baseball* Stand

- **Bottom board:** 5¼" (13.2 cm) square

- **Top board:** 3¾" (9.5 cm) square

- **Dowels:** 3" (7.5 cm) long

Dimensions for Basketball Stand

- **Bottom board:** 10" (25.5 cm) square

- **Top board:** 8½" (21.8 cm) square

- **Dowels:** 5" (12.5 cm) long

*Use only three dowels for baseball stand. Position two dowels on one edge of top board as directed in steps 3 to 5. Position the third dowel on opposite edge, 1" (2.5 cm) from edge and centered.

RICHFIELD
HIGH SCHOOL
RICHFIELD, MINNESOTA
STUDENT

002969

Decoupage
SPORTS GIFTS

Decoupage is a very simple embellishment technique that yields impressive results. Transform clear glass plates, picture frames, wooden boxes, or plain wooden plaques into keepsakes that commemorate a specific event or player.

To celebrate a state championship, make a decoupage plate with the team photo and newspaper headlines that have been copied onto high-quality paper. Team colors can be painted into the background. A wooden box can be embellished as a holder for baseball trading cards or as a keepsake box to hold awards from personal sports achievements, ticket stubs, and other sports paraphernalia.

Decoupage glass Plate

MATERIALS

❖Photographs and other embellishments cut from high-quality paper ❖Clear glass plate ❖Decoupage medium; brush or sponge applicator ❖Sponge or brayer ❖Acrylic paints and brush or small piece of natural sea sponge for applying paints ❖Aerosol acrylic paint, optional ❖Aerosol clear acrylic sealer

1 Trace the plate on a piece of paper; plan placement of embellishments. Clean back of plate thoroughly, using glass cleaner and lint-free rag; place plate facedown on table.

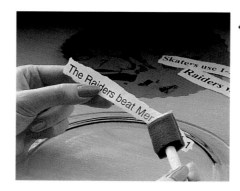

2 Apply a thin layer of decoupage medium to front of foreground embellishment, using sponge applicator, brush, or finger. Position embellishment on back of the plate; smooth out with dampened sponge or a brayer. (Any excess decoupage medium around the edges of the embellishment will not show when plate is painted.)

Decoupage box or Plaque

MATERIALS

❖Unfinished wooden box or plaque ❖Acrylic craft paints in desired colors ❖Photographs and other embellishments cut from high-quality paper ❖Decoupage medium; brush or sponge applicator ❖Brayer or sponge ❖Aerosol clear acrylic sealer

1 Paint box or plaque in team colors, using acrylic craft paints. Allow to dry.

2 Apply thin layer of decoupage medium to the back of the background embellishment, using brush, sponge applicator, or finger. Position the embellishment on the lid of box or plaque; smooth out with brayer or dampened sponge. Wipe away excess decoupage medium from around the edges of the embellishment, using damp cloth.

3 Continue applying embellishments as desired, working from foreground to background if the embellishments are layered. Allow to dry. Apply a thin coat of decoupage medium to the back of the embellishments as a sealer; allow to dry.

4 Apply lightest color of acrylic paint to the plate, using sea sponge; apply sparingly. Apply remaining layers of paint, finishing with darkest color. If desired, paint back of plate a solid color, using aerosol acrylic paint. Allow to dry.

5 Apply light coat of aerosol acrylic sealer to back of plate; allow to dry. Apply second coat.

3 Continue applying embellishments as desired, working from background to foreground if embellishments are layered. Allow to dry. Apply thin coat of decoupage medium to top of embellishments as a sealer; allow to dry.

4 Apply light coat of aerosol acrylic sealer to lid of box or plaque; allow to dry. Apply second coat.

☞ *This technique may be used on a stained and finished box or plaque as well as on a painted one.*

FRAMED Sports posters

Posters and poster advertisements are wonderful mementos of races run or favorite sports teams. Framing posters gives them lasting appeal and is easier to do yourself than you might think.

Many frame shops and craft stores carry ready-made frames and framing units called sectionals. Sectionals are lengths of frame molding packaged as sets with two pieces of equal length. You buy one package to match the length of the poster and one to match the width.

Before you begin framing, mount your poster to foam-core board, using spray adhesive, or have it dry-mounted to the board at a frame store. Have the store cut glass or plexiglass to fit your frame. Glass or plexiglass can also be purchased in home-improvement stores.

If desired, personalize inexpensive posters by adding flat, paper embellishments, using double-sided tape or paper glue. For example, a basketball poster could be embellished with ticket stubs, the front of a program, or an autographed photograph. A poster from a marathon could have a photo of the runner, a piece of torn finish-line tape, and the number that the runner wore in the race.

Wooden sectional Frame

MATERIALS

❖One pair wooden sectionals, the length of the poster ❖One pair wooden sectionals, the width of the poster ❖Wood glue ❖Glass or plexiglass; cut to fit frame ❖Poster, mounted on foam-core board ❖Putty knife or screwdriver ❖Sawtooth picture hanger and nails, or two screw eyes and picture wire

☞ *Stain raw ends of frame sectionals before assembling frame to conceal any corners that aren't perfectly matched.*

1 Place all pieces of sectional frame sectionals on large, flat work area. Join one corner of frame at a time, with frame facedown on work surface.

2 Apply a small amount of wood glue to one corner joint; then insert plastic plug from kit into the corner from the back side of the frame. If necessary, gently tap plug into corner until tight, using a hammer.

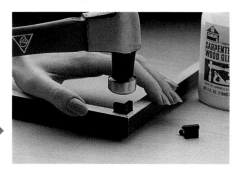

3 Repeat with third and fourth sections of the frame. Allow to dry.

4 Clean both sides of glass thoroughly, using glass cleaner and a lint-free cloth. Position glass over the mounted poster, with edges even. Position frame over glass. Check the glass for lint or fingerprints. Slide fingers under mounted poster, and turn frame over.

5 Secure poster in place, using the glazing points included with kit. Insert glazing points into the frame on all sides, pushing them into place with putty knife or screwdriver.

6 Position the sawtooth nail hanger in the middle of the back of the top frame section; secure with nails. If using screw eyes, position one on each side of frame back 5" (12.5 cm) from top of poster. Secure picture wire as in step 6, opposite.

1 Place all pieces of frame sectionals facedown on large, flat work area. Insert one corner angle unit from the kit into the end of the frame channel of bottom section of frame. Make sure thick piece with screws is on top of the thin piece.

2 Slide vertical side section of frame over angle unit until mitered corners meet. Tighten screws, holding the mitered corner tightly so it stays aligned. Repeat steps 1 and 2 to secure the second side section of the frame.

MATERIALS

❖One pair metal sectionals, the length of the poster ❖One pair metal sectionals, the width of the poster ❖Glass or plexiglass, cut to fit frame ❖Poster, mounted on foam-core board ❖Screwdriver ❖Picture wire

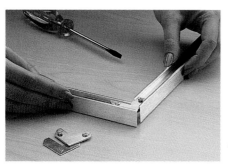

3 Clean both sides of glass thoroughly, using glass cleaner and a lint-free cloth. Position glass over mounted poster, with edges even. Check the glass for lint or fingerprints. Slide poster and glass, bottom end first, into frame.

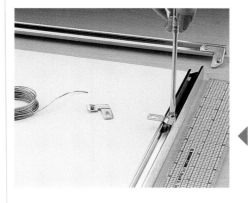

4 Insert hangers from kit into the channels of the side sections of the frame, positioning them 5" (12.5 cm) from top of the poster. Tighten screws.

5 Repeat steps 1 and 2 to secure top section of the frame. Insert spring clips from kit between mounted poster and frame, if necessary to secure the poster tightly in the frame.

6 Thread picture wire two or three times through one poster hanger; twist the end. Repeat at opposite side, leaving some slack; wire should be 2" to 3" (5 to 7.5 cm) from top of frame when hung.

15

PUZZLE
Scrapbook

Scrapbooks or photo albums are terrific ways to follow and record an individual's sports career or even a successful season. By keeping track and faithfully clipping articles and taking photographs, you can create a precious and personal gift for someone.

Highlight this thoughtful gift with a creative presentation of a filled scrapbook or photo album. Secure a photograph of the featured individual in the center of a book or album cover, using a glue stick or aerosol adhesive. Protect the photo with a piece of acetate, if desired. Surround the photo with pieces from a jigsaw puzzle that represents the sport on which you are focusing. For a skier, choose a mountain puzzle; for a hunter, select a field or game bird; for a baseball player, purchase a puzzle with a baseball theme. Slightly overlap puzzle pieces in two or three layers or place them randomly on the book, securing pieces with hot glue or craft glue. If desired, complete small portions of the puzzle.

SPORTS
Photo frames

Make simple and innovative photo frames to accent a favorite photo of your athlete in action. You can embellish plain purchased frames with paint pens, decals, headlines or pictures cut from newspapers and magazines, or sports paraphernalia. Make a general sports frame or one to commemorate a specific event, such as winning a marathon or tournament.

Convert inexpensive used or discount sports items into creative photo frames. Children's ice skates or high-top tennis shoes make interesting holders for photos. Or use ski goggles or an underwater face mask as a frame.

Embellished Frame

MATERIALS

❖Plain photo frame ❖Pictures or headlines cut from magazines or newspapers ❖Clear-drying craft glue or rubber cement ❖Small bowl ❖Sponge ❖Aerosol clear acrylic sealer ❖Sports decals or appliqués, if desired

1 Disassemble the frame; set the glass and backing aside.

2 Thin a small amount of craft glue with an equal amount of water in bowl. (Rubber cement does not require thinning.) Apply a light coating of glue to backs of paper cutouts, using finger.

Ice skate or tennis shoe Frame

MATERIALS

❖Small ice skate or high-top tennis shoe ❖Ruler; pen ❖Wood block or heavy cardboard ❖Mat knife ❖Clear plastic or acetate ❖Athletic tape or duct tape ❖Photograph

1 Mark outline of photo frame opening on ankle portion of skate in desired shape, using ruler and pen.

2 Place wood block or cardboard inside skate for use as a cutting surface. Cut just along the outside of the marked outline, using mat knife.

3 Position cutouts on frame as desired, smoothing air bubbles out with finger.

Wipe away excess glue, using damp sponge. Allow to dry. Apply one or two coats of aerosol acrylic sealer to frame. Allow to dry. ▶

4 Secure decals or appliqués to the frame, using unthinned craft glue.

☞ *Cut items from magazines or newspapers on cutting surface using mat knife to ensure clean edges.*

☞ *Apply aerosol clear acrylic sealer to newspaper or magazine items and allow to dry prior to gluing for added durability.*

3 Cut piece of plastic large enough to cover frame opening. Secure plastic inside skate, over opening, using tape. Position photograph inside skate so it shows through the opening; secure with tape. ▼

4 Hang skate frame on wall, using laces.

☞ *Tuck sweatsock inside skate or shoe to conceal back of photo, if desired.*

☞ *Add further embellishment to skate or shoe, such as a name or important date, using paint pens. Use dimensional paint to outline frame opening.*

Golf ball Frame

MATERIALS

❖Sturdy, solid wood table frame ❖Drill and ⅛" drill bit ❖Golf balls ❖Drywall screws, long enough to go through frame plus ½" (1.3 cm) into ball ❖Screwdriver

1 Determine number of golf balls to place along bottom of frame. Mark the placement for the center of each ball, using pencil. Drill pilot holes at markings; drill corresponding holes into the balls.

2 Screw drywall screws into pilot holes from back of frame, just until tips of screws protrude on front of frame.

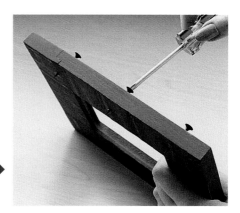

3 Place pilot hole for golf ball over one screw tip. Continue screwing drywall screw through the frame and into golf ball. Repeat with remaining golf balls. ▼

☞ For a large wall frame, position golf balls all around perimeter.

☞ For additional embellishment, secure golf tees to front of frame, using hot glue.

Goggles or face mask Frame

MATERIALS

❖Face mask or goggles ❖Photo enlarged to fill goggles or mask ❖Mat knife; cutting surface ❖Aerosol adhesive or glue stick

1 Cut photo to fit on front of face mask, using mat knife. Secure photo on front of mask, using aerosol adhesive or glue stick. ▼

☞ Stand frame on desk or shelf instead of hanging it.

PERSONALIZED
Trading card book

Three-ring binders are great tools for organizing trading cards—much better than the old shoebox method of storage. Purchase a plain, inexpensive binder and fill it with plastic card-holder pages, available in sports stores and trading card stores.

Personalize and tailor the binder with wrapping paper in a team color, or with a sports-related motif. Sports posters could even be used to wrap the binder. Further embellish the binder with sports stickers or writing, using a permanent-ink marker.

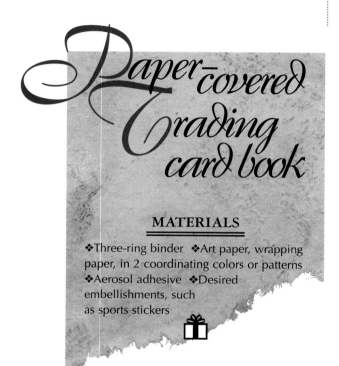

Paper-covered Trading card book

MATERIALS

❖Three-ring binder ❖Art paper, wrapping paper, in 2 coordinating colors or patterns ❖Aerosol adhesive ❖Desired embellishments, such as sports stickers

1 Cut the paper 1" (2.5 cm) larger than the opened binder on all sides. Place the paper facedown on work surface. Apply a generous coat of aerosol adhesive to back of the paper.

2 Place spine of binder in center of paper; press gently. Working from spine to edge of cover, smooth one side of paper over front cover of the binder. Repeat for back of binder. ▼

3 Fold excess paper from sides of front and back covers to inside of book; press and smooth paper to the inside of covers. Cut notches in paper at top and bottom of book at the spine.

4 Fold excess paper from tops and bottoms of the cover to inside of the book; fold in corners as you would when wrapping a gift. Press and smooth the paper to inside of cover.

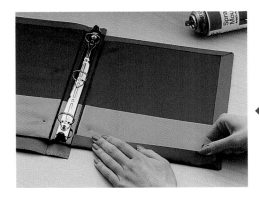

5 Cut second paper into two sheets with dimensions ¼" (6 mm) smaller than inside of covers on three outer edges. Spray backs of sheets with aerosol adhesive. Press sheets to inside of front and back covers. Embellish front cover of book as desired.

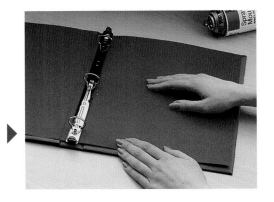

Go Tech

swimmers ... **ped to saw**

Skippers, Edina, Ho ... re section favorites

and most of
... high school
... taken literally.
The end of the regular season brings with it an end to resis-
tance training. That means
Skipper swimmers can say good-
bye to the drag suits they've
worn almost all season.
Swimmers have less charita-
ble names for them, such
"death suits," or the

meets is not a new tactic — the
Minnetonka boys have done it
for years — but ditching the drag
suits in favor of more traditional
swim wear can result in a sud-
den burst of speed in the section
and state meets, when swimmers need it most.
"Wearing the suits can
count for two or three
onds per

season, but they
sacrifice their long-ra
to get it."
One of those goals is win
the state team championship
that happens, it would
netonka's sixth

High.
Tonka, ranked third in
be among th

SPORTS MEMORABILIA
Shadow boxes

Showcase favorite sports mementos in shadow boxes. These deep-sided frames allow you to mount dimensional items like golf balls, hockey pucks, fishing lures, track medals, and even Little League baseball gloves. Create a collage using multiple items, including game tickets or programs, photographs, and autographs.

Small shadow boxes are available in craft stores, frame shops, and home decorating stores. You can mount items yourself, following the mounting tips on pages 30 and 31. For larger items, most frame shops can custom-make large shadow boxes. If you are familiar with framing techniques, you can mount the items and finish the box yourself, or have the frame shop complete the entire project.

Before mounting items in the box, arrange all items to be framed on a sheet of craft paper cut to the display dimensions of the box. Outline the items on the paper to record placement. Refer to the paper when mounting items in the box.

Stitch Mounting

MATERIALS

❖Item to be mounted ❖Needle
❖Monofilament fishing line or thread that matches item ❖Thimble

1 Determine several locations where article can be supported. Using threaded needle and thimble, secure item, taking about three stitches through mounting board at each support location.

2 Knot thread and conceal it behind mounted item.

☞ *Use this technique for very small items or items made of fabric.*

Hinge Mounting

MATERIALS

❖Item to be mounted ❖Linen framer's tape

☞ *Use this technique for photographs, tickets, programs, or other paper items.*

1 Cut a 1" to 2" (2.5 to 5 cm) strip of framer's tape, depending on the size and weight of the item to be mounted. Fold back ¼" to ½" (6 mm to 1.3 cm) of tape, adhesive side out.

2 Place item to be mounted facedown on a flat surface. Moisten short side of strip and secure at upper edge on back of item as shown, positioning the tape with folded side ⅛" (3 mm) from the edge of item. Repeat at opposite end of item. Position as many strips as necessary to secure item.

3 Moisten the remainder of the strips; secure item to be mounted inside shadow box as desired.

Silicone glue Mounting

MATERIALS

❖Item to be mounted ❖Clear silicone glue

1 Secure item to be mounted with a bead of silicone glue. Allow the glue to cure for 24 hours before hanging shadow box. ▼

☞ *Silicone glue stays flexible and can be removed without damaging the item.*

☞ *Use this technique for lightweight, bulky items, such as fishing lures, golf balls, or medals.*

Hook & loop Mounting

MATERIALS

❖Item to be mounted ❖Self-adhesive hook and loop tape

1 Cut short strips of hook and loop tape. Secure one side of tape to the shadow box and the other side to item to be mounted. Mount item by pressing both sides of tape together.

☞ *Use this technique for flat-sided, lightweight items.*

IDEAS *for* Outdoor sports

There is a wide variety of practical gifts for the outdoor sports enthusiast. Specialty stores and large sporting goods stores enable you to one-stop shop, regardless of the sport for which you're buying.

Bikers will appreciate a cushioned bicycle seat, a bike chain and lock, biking gloves, tire repair kit, a water bottle with holder, a horn or bell, reflectors, or a small bike tool kit. Arrange these items in a new bike helmet.

If you know an avid snow skier, fill a ski stocking cap with a leather boda, hand and feet warmers, polarized sunglasses or goggles, ski wax, and a lift pass to their favorite slopes or a permit for a specific cross-country ski trail.

RUNNER'S *Wallets*

A common problem for joggers, bikers, or anyone who works out in a gym is where to keep money or keys while exercising. Because of their level of activity, they need a secure place to carry these items without being inhibited by them.

Runner's wallets, with hook and loop closures such as Velcro®, are inexpensive and easy to make. You can even purchase cases for keys that fasten to the laces on your shoes. Or purchase the elements for making a case to solve the where-to-put-my-money problem. For example, a nylon wallet with a hook and loop closure can be easily fastened over a washable nylon web belt; both are available in sporting goods stores.

Nylon wallet Pouch

MATERIALS

❖Nylon fabric in desired color ❖Needle or sewing machine, and contrasting thread ❖Fusible web, ¼" (6 mm) wide ❖Self-adhesive hook and loop tape

1 Cut piece of nylon fabric at least 9" × 3¼" (23 × 8.2 cm). This will make a pouch big enough to hold a credit card, a few dollar bills, and a key. Cut fabric slightly larger if a roomier pouch is desired.

2 Fold ¼" (6 mm) of short ends of the fabric over, wrong sides together. Stitch folded edges in place.

Ankle or wrist Wallet

MATERIALS

❖*Nylon Wallet Pouch,* above ❖Hook and loop wrist band, available in sporting goods stores

1 Secure pouch to wrist band by folding open flap of pouch over the band, then pressing hook and loop pieces of pouch together.

3 Place fabric right side up on flat surface. Fold 3¼" (8.2 cm) of piece lengthwise over rest of piece, with right sides together. Stitch a ¼" (6 mm) margin on each side of folded section to make a pouch.

4 Turn pouch right side out. Fold ¼" (6 mm) of each side of top flap in. Cut two 1¾" (4.5 cm) strips of fusible web. Secure folded sides of flap, using fusible web, according to manufacturer's instructions.

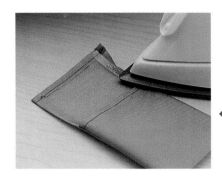

5 Cut 2½" × ⅜" (6.5 × 1 cm) piece of hook and loop tape. Secure hook portion to flap of pouch and loop portion to pouch so they meet when flap is closed.

☞ *After folding edges of fabric over, press them with an iron before stitching.*

☞ *Secure strips of self-adhesive reflective tape to wallets for safety.*

1 Stitch the back of the pouch to the wristband.

Sweatband Wallet

MATERIALS

❖*Nylon Wallet Pouch, above* ❖Terry cloth wristband ❖Needle and thread

PRESENTATION IDEAS *for* Sports equipment

Sports equipment essentials are always good stocking stuffers and gifts for the active sports enthusiast. Give these items an interesting presentation to add to the thoughtfulness of the gifts.

A 10-quart (9.46 L) plastic cooler is the perfect size for taking to the courts, especially if you fill it with a "six-pack" combination of tennis ball cans and water bottles. Bottles of a sports drink or bottled water are also good fillers. If desired, embellish bottle tops with stickers or hand-painted balls.

Sports socks are always a welcome gift. Roll up three different colors of socks into balls, and place them in an empty tennis ball can. Wool hiking socks can be filled with small items, like energy bars, a pocket knife, a compass, sunscreen, or other small items.

Spray the inside of an egg carton with green paint, and fill it with monogrammed golf balls. You can embellish the carton with golf tees, if desired.

DECORATED
Bike helmets

Bike helmets are practical pieces of safety equipment, but that doesn't mean they have to be boring. Decorated helmets are popular, especially with young people, but their cost can be prohibitive. Why not get a reasonably priced, solid-colored helmet and embellish it yourself?

Simple painting techniques, using an oil-based automobile paint for durability, can be used to decorate helmets. Add holographic or brightly colored stickers, or car-detailing stripes, to the helmet, if desired. Reflective tape can also be cut into designs, such as lightning bolts, and attached to the helmet.

Embellished Helmet

MATERIALS

❖Plain bike helmet ❖Painter's masking tape ❖Newspaper or large plastic bag ❖Oil-based aerosol automobile paint, in desired color ❖Stickers or car-detailing accent stripes, optional ❖Aerosol clear acrylic sealer, optional

1 Tape off areas to be painted with the desired design, such as lightning bolts, using painter's masking tape. Mask the rest of helmet with newspaper or a plastic bag; secure with tape.

2 Apply several light coats of paint to exposed area of helmet. Allow to dry. Remove tape and newspaper or plastic bag. Embellish the rest of the helmet as desired with stickers or car-detailing stripes. Apply one or two light coats of aerosol acrylic sealer to helmet, if desired. Allow to dry.

☞ *Pearlescent, metallic paint works very well for this treatment.*

Spatter-painted Helmet

MATERIALS

❖Plain bike helmet ❖Painter's masking tape ❖Acrylic gloss enamel paints, in desired colors ❖Craft paintbrush ❖Aerosol clear acrylic sealer, optional

1 Mask any areas on the helmet you do not want painted, using masking tape. Place helmet on newspaper-lined work surface.

☞ *Stuff tissue paper into vent holes from the inside of helmet to prevent paint from getting inside.*

☞ *Use this technique on a helmet that has a design spray-painted on it, as above, if desired.*

☞ *If necessary, dilute paint with water for easier spattering.*

1 Apply first paint color to helmet in slightly curved brush strokes. Allow to dry; clean the brush.

Freehand swirl Helmet

MATERIALS

❖Plain bike helmet ❖Acrylic gloss enamel paints, in 3 colors ❖#4 round artist's brush ❖Aerosol clear acrylic sealer, optional

2 Apply the second color in curving brush strokes about half the length of the first color's, using less pressure on the brush so strokes are not as wide. Allow some strokes to overlap those of the first color. Allow to dry; clean the brush.

3 Apply third color in curving strokes about half the length of the second color's, using just the tip of the brush. Allow some strokes to overlap the first color. Allow to dry. Apply one or two light coats of aerosol acrylic sealer to helmet, if desired. Allow to dry. ▼

2 Wet the brush with paint, and tap brush against a pencil to spatter paint onto the helmet. Repeat with as many other colors as desired. Allow to dry. Apply one or two light coats of aerosol acrylic sealer to helmet, if desired. Allow to dry.

GIFTS *for the* Horse lover

Horse owners and horse enthusiasts enjoy gifts that relate to their favorite hobby. A trip to a saddle shop or western store will provide you with many items you might want to give.

Fill a galvanized bucket with items for the horse, such as a brush and curry comb, horse treats, and a bug repellent for its stall. You might also include saddle soap or other supplies for cleaning gear.

An inexpensive straw hat makes a nice container for a string tie, Western jewelry, or a colorful bandanna for the rider. Add a book on horses or a magazine, along with a year's subscription to the magazine.

HIKING & FISHING Vests

Whether outdoor enthusiasts are hiking in the hills or wading through a trout stream, vests provide a convenient, hands-free way for them to carry miscellaneous gear.

Vests should have lots of pockets for carrying assorted items. Canvas vests for serious hiking and vests with mesh backs for hot weather are available at most outdoor or sports stores.

Give the vest as a gift by itself, or equip it with many of the items needed for enjoyment of these outdoor sports. A hiker may appreciate a bottle of insect repellent, notepad and pen for field notes, bird or insect identification book, pocket knife, small flashlight, or energy bar. Include a book or subscription to a hiking or fishing magazine. On the following pages, you will find tips for all the items necessary to outfit a fishing vest.

Outfitting a trout-fishing Vest

Essential Equipment:

1) Landing net, with a short handle and cotton mesh netting 2) Fly box filled with assorted flies 3) Forceps or needlenose pliers for removing hooks and flattening barbs for catch-and-release fishing 4) Line clipper or fingernail clippers for cutting lines 5) Split shot in assorted sizes for sinking flies 6) Silicone floatant paste, liquid, or spray to keep dry flies floating 7) Tippet material in several diameters for rebuilding leaders 8) Swiss army knife for an assortment of tasks

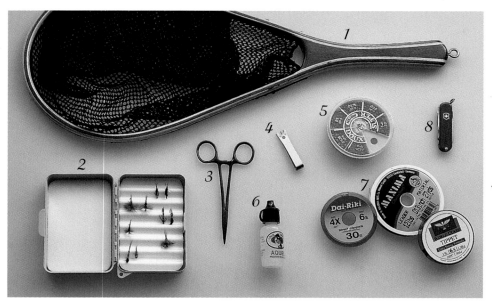

Optional Equipment:

❖Fishing line ❖Water thermometer ❖Insect repellant ❖Creel made of canvas or wicker for holding fish ❖Tape measure

Tips for Converting a Plain Hiking Vest into a Fishing Vest:

☞ *Stitch D-rings to vest, using a piece of cotton webbing as an anchor. Attach one to back of collar for landing net and two on chest for clippers and other frequently used items.*

☞ *Secure a small square of fleece to chest pocket of vest, using needle and thread or fabric glue. The wool fleece is used to hold frequently used flies.*

Hiking & camping IDEAS

Since hiking and camping are such popular activities, it's easy to find quick and fun gift items for people who like the outdoors. A trip to an outdoor or sports store will provide you with all the items you could wish for in a variety of price ranges.

Fill a day pack with assorted hiking necessities and niceties, such as a water bottle, hiking socks, maps and guide books, a small first aid kit, compass, sunscreen, and energy bars. A fanny pack can be equipped as an emergency kit by filling it with a first aid book and kit, an elastic bandage, antiseptic ointment, cleansing pads and ointments, small flashlight, waterproof matches, and energy bars.

Give the camper a "mess kit." Bundle up a metal camping plate, cup, and flatware with a bag of dehydrated camping food, using a bandanna. A cook pot can be filled with assorted dehydrated food items, biodegradable soap, and waterproof matches. You could even include a "S'mores Emergency Kit" with marshmallows, chocolate bars, and graham crackers.

PERSONALIZED
Clothing
& towels

Personalized clothing displaying a favorite team or sport can be made at a fraction of the cost of that found at sporting goods stores. Create one-of-a-kind caps, T-shirts, sweatshirts, shorts, sweatpants, scarves, or socks for the sports enthusiasts that you know. Embellish towels for use on the field or in the locker room, too.

On the following pages, you'll find simple techniques for embellishing a sweatshirt and a sports towel, and creating a tee-holder golf hat, using items that can usually be found in craft stores. Use these techniques on any article of clothing you desire.

Fusible transfer Sweatshirt

MATERIALS

❖Sweatshirt in desired size and color
❖Polyester felt in desired color ❖Fusible transfers for emblems and letters for desired sport or team ❖Sheets of fusible web

☞ *Add some fusible transfers without felt backing to shirt, as well.*

1 Prewash sweatshirt and felt according to the manufacturer's instructions to allow for shrinkage.

2 Fuse transfers to felt, then apply fusible web to back of felt, according to the manufacturer's instructions. Leave paper backing on web.

3 Cut emblems and letters from felt, leaving a border of felt outlining each emblem or letter.

4 Remove the paper backing from cutouts, and iron onto sweatshirt in desired position, according to the manufacturer's instructions.

Golf tee Hat

MATERIALS

❖White, adjustable-size cap ❖³/8" (1 cm) white grosgrain ribbon ❖Twelve small nail-head tacks, ¹/4" (6 mm) diameter ❖Five golf tees ❖Iron-on golf appliqué, if desired

1 Cut the ribbon long enough to encircle front half of the hat, about 14" (35.5 cm). Center ribbon along front of cap, positioning top edge of the ribbon 1" (2.5 cm) from bill of cap.

2 Center a tee vertically under ribbon in the center of front of cap. Secure ribbon to cap on one side of tee with nail-head tack, by piercing ribbon and cap with points on back of tack and bending points inside cap. Pull ribbon snugly around tee; secure a second nail head on opposite side of tee.

1 Prewash towel according to manufacturer's instructions.

2 Place the desired number of appliqués along the band of towel that has no nap. Iron the appliqués onto the towel according to the manufacturer's instructions.

Sports Towel

MATERIALS

❖Towel in desired color ❖Iron-on sports appliqués, such as baseballs, footballs, soccer balls, etc.

☞ *For a more secure hold on towel, use fusible web that has been cut to a slightly smaller size than appliqués. Or sew appliqués on towel.*

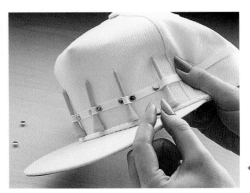

3 Secure a third nail head approximately 1" (2.5 cm) to the right of the second nail head. Place a second tee under the ribbon, and secure as before. Repeat on right side with two more nail heads and one more tee. Repeat entire process on left side of cap.

4 Secure the remaining two nail heads on opposite ends of ribbon. Trim the ends of the ribbon as desired.

5 Iron appliqué onto bill of cap according to the manufacturer's instructions.

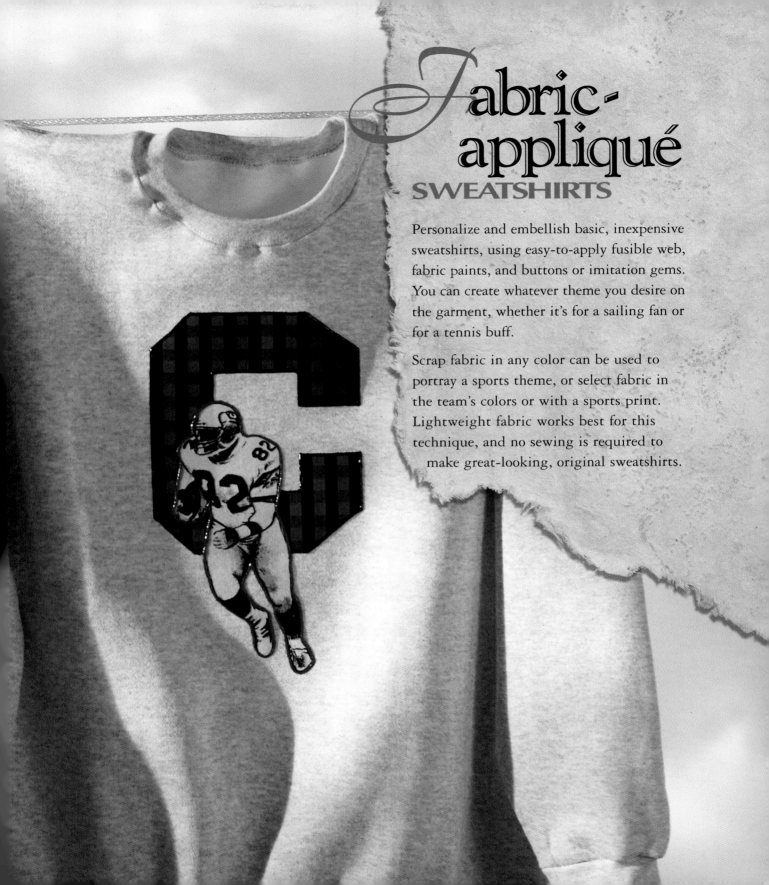

Fabric-appliqué
SWEATSHIRTS

Personalize and embellish basic, inexpensive sweatshirts, using easy-to-apply fusible web, fabric paints, and buttons or imitation gems. You can create whatever theme you desire on the garment, whether it's for a sailing fan or for a tennis buff.

Scrap fabric in any color can be used to portray a sports theme, or select fabric in the team's colors or with a sports print. Lightweight fabric works best for this technique, and no sewing is required to make great-looking, original sweatshirts.

Fabric-appliqué Sweatshirt

MATERIALS

❖Sweatshirt in desired color ❖Scrap fabric in desired colors and patterns ❖Sheets of fusible web ❖Stencils, optional ❖Lead pencil ❖Dimensional fabric paint

1 Prewash sweatshirt and fabric separately according to manufacturer's instructions. Do not use soap or fabric softener, or appliqués will not adhere properly.

2 Determine the design for the sweatshirt, including any lettering or design motifs. You may want to sketch it out on a piece of scrap paper. Determine the size of designs by measuring the space available on the sweatshirt. Cutting designs and letters out of scrap paper or roughly cutting them from patterned fabric and placing them on the sweatshirt is helpful for estimating.

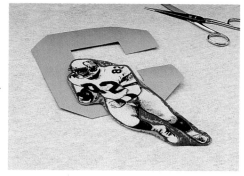

3 Cut pieces of fabric and fusible web slightly larger than the letters or design motifs you plan to use. Following manufacturer's instructions, apply fusible web to back of fabric, leaving paper backing on web.

4 Mark outline of letters or design motifs lightly on fronts of fabric pieces, using pencil; use stencils, if desired, or freehand draw your designs. Cut letters and design motifs from fabric just inside marked lines.

5 Place cutouts on the sweatshirt to make sure you are satisfied with their placement. If desired, mark placement on shirt, using pencil. Remove the backing from cutouts and iron onto the sweatshirt one at a time, according to manufacturer's instructions.

6 Apply paint around outlines of appliqué designs to conceal unfinished edges. Allow to dry.

Fabric paint Gem accents

MATERIALS

❖Completed *Fabric Appliqué Sweatshirt,* left ❖Dimensional fabric paint ❖Imitation gems

🎁

1 Apply small pools of paint slightly larger than the diameter of gems randomly on sweatshirt. Press gems into paint. Allow to dry.

☞ *Use buttons with sports motifs on them. If necessary, cut off button shanks with wire snips before securing buttons to shirt.*

Remote control
T-SHIRT

Create a fun and useful gift for your favorite television jock by making a T-shirt, sweatshirt, or vest specifically for holding the remote control. That way the remote will always be within easy reach when it's time to switch to a different ball game.

Pockets can be easily stitched on a purchased team sweatshirt, or for a no-sew alternative, use fusible web to iron pockets onto your garment. Instead of buying a specific team's shirt, select a plain T-shirt in the desired color. Choose pocket fabric in the same color or in a coordinating color. Then embellish the shirt as desired, using fabric paints or iron-on appliqués.

Remote control T-shirt

MATERIALS

❖T-shirt in desired color ❖Pocket fabric in desired color ❖Fusible web, 3/8" (1 cm) width ❖Fabric paint and iron-on appliqués, if desired

1 Prewash the T-shirt and pocket fabric according to manufacturer's instructions; do not use fabric softener.

2 Measure width, length, and height of remote control. Cut fabric so its length equals the length of the remote control. The fabric width should be at least equal to the width of the remote control plus two times its height. Add 2" (5 cm) to the width for seams.

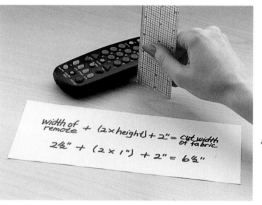

Width of remote + (2 × height) + 2" = Cut width of fabric

$2\frac{1}{2}" + (2 \times 1") + 2" = 6\frac{1}{2}"$

☞ *The measurements given in step 2 will allow for a snug fit for the remote control with approximately 1" (2.5 cm) of it sticking out of the top of the pocket. You may add more to the width and length for a roomier pocket, if desired.*

3 Fold ½" (1.3 cm) of fabric over on the wrong side of fabric at top and bottom; press with iron. Fold ½" (1.3 cm) of fabric over on the wrong side at the sides; press with iron.

4 Cut piece of fusible web to the width of top of pocket. Insert the web under seam at top of pocket. Trim web, if necessary, so it is concealed by seam. Press with iron to fuse. ▼

5 Position pocket on shirt in desired position; secure with pins. Cut one piece of fusible web to the width of the bottom of pocket; cut two pieces to the length of pocket sides. Place web strips between pocket and shirt under seams at bottom and sides. Trim web, if necessary, so it is not exposed to inside of pocket. Press with iron to fuse. ◀

☞ *Embellish the pocket and shirt as desired with fabric paint and iron-on appliqués.*

☞ *For durability, reinforce pocket by stitching a triangle at upper corners.*

☞ *Embellish the shirt with more than one pocket—one for the TV remote control and one for the VCR remote control.*

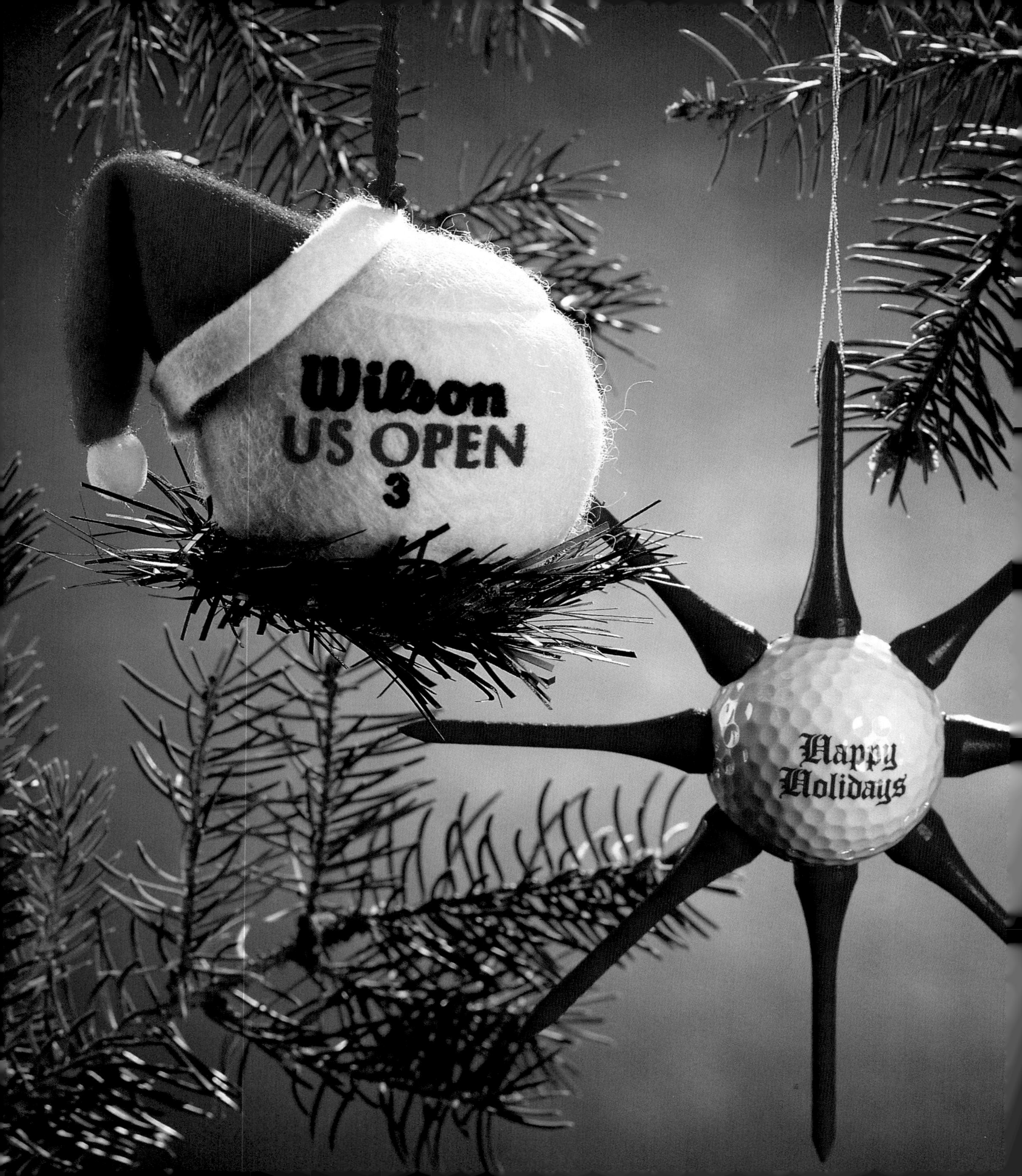
Wilson
US OPEN
3
Happy
Holidays

HOLIDAY
*S*ports
ornaments

Holiday ornaments are whimsical, simple gifts for sports enthusiasts. Whether you use actual sports gear or miniature reproductions, you can make a number of creative decorations for the Christmas tree.

Put a red felt Santa hat on a tennis ball. Make a star out of a golf ball and golf tees. Look through sports stores or craft stores for small items with a sports theme. You can even find table tennis balls that look like basketballs, soccer balls, or baseballs.

All-sport Ornament

MATERIALS

❖ Three table tennis balls resembling a basketball, a baseball, and a soccer ball ❖ Drill and ¹/₈" drill bit ❖ 22-gauge or 24-gauge paddle floral wire and wire cutter ❖ Needlenose pliers ❖ Artificial pine garland ❖ Ribbon

☞ *Substitute golf balls for table tennis balls.*

1 Drill two holes, directly opposite one another, in top and bottom of each ball. Cut 8" (20.5 cm) piece of floral wire. Insert the wire through holes in each ball, stacking balls. Bend 1" (2.5 cm) of top end of wire into the loop for hanger, using pliers; insert end into the ball. Repeat at bottom end of wire.

2 Wind two pieces of garland around wire between the balls.

3 Tie ribbon to the ends of wire. Trim as desired.

Santa Ball

MATERIALS

❖ Tennis ball ❖ Drill and ¹/₈" drill bit ❖ 20-gauge paddle floral wire; wire cutter ❖ Needlenose pliers ❖ 3³/₄" (9.5 cm) square red felt ❖ 7" × ³/₈" (18 × 1 cm) strip white felt ❖ Small white pom-pom ❖ Hot glue gun and glue sticks ❖ One or two small pieces artificial pine bough

1 Drill two holes, directly opposite one another, in top and bottom of tennis ball. Cut 5" (12.5 cm) piece of floral wire. Insert wire through the ball from top hole to bottom hole. Bend 1" (2.5 cm) of top end of wire into loop for hanger, using pliers; insert end into ball. Bend bottom end of wire into loop, pressing loop flat against ball.

1 Drill hole ³⁄₈" (1 cm) from the pointed end of one golf tee; drill completely through for a hanger.

2 Insert tee in piece of foam. Apply small drop of glue to top of tee; place golf ball upside down on tee, pressing gently. Allow glue to set.

3 Remove tee and ball from the foam. Insert the second tee in the foam. Apply drop of glue to tee; place the golf ball on the tee, so second tee is directly opposite first tee. Allow glue to set.

MATERIALS

❖Golf balls ❖Eight golf tees ❖Drill and ¹⁄₁₆" drill bit ❖Piece of foam ❖Jewelry glue or rubber cement ❖Gold or silver aerosol acrylic paint, optional

4 Continue securing tees to ball in this manner until all tees are evenly spaced and radiate in a straight line around ball. Paint star with gold or silver paint, if desired.

2 Fold red felt square in half diagonally with right side in. Stitch one edge of the folded felt together with ¹⁄₈" (3 mm) margin. Turn piece right side out; poke tip of hat up with a pencil. Trim bottom corner from hat, rounding edges.

3 Secure strip of white felt around bottom edge of hat, using hot glue; trim felt strip so there is only ¹⁄₄" (6 mm) overlap that is aligned with seam of hat. Secure pom-pom to tip of hat, using hot glue.

4 Secure hat to top of ball at an angle next to wire loop, using hot glue. Bend tip of hat down and secure to side of hat. Secure pine bough to bottom of ball, concealing bottom loop.

Tee-time CLOCK

Let your favorite golfer know that it's always tee time with this easy-to-make clock. Inexpensive, plain wooden case clocks can be easily found, and multicolored tees add a touch of whimsy.

If desired, you can secure a golf ball to the top of one tee, using jewelry glue or rubber cement. Use a monogrammed ball or one commemorating a special place or event.

Tee-time Clock

MATERIALS

❖Plain, wooden case desk clock ❖Drill and 5/32" drill bit ❖Masking tape ❖25 to 30 colored golf tees ❖Rubber mallet ❖Wood glue, optional

1 Mark desired placement of tees on clock face, sides, and top, using a pencil. Placement may be random or uniform.

2 Wrap a piece of masking tape around drill bit with edge of tape ⅜" (1 cm) from tip of bit. Drill holes at each marked point, varying the angles of the holes. Stop drilling each hole when edge of tape meets surface of wood.

3 Insert tees in holes. Gently tap tees with rubber mallet to secure them. If tees are loose, secure them in holes, using wood glue.

☞ A piece of masking tape placed on the clock at the location to be drilled will prevent possible splintering at edges of drill holes.

☞ If embellishing a wall clock, you may want to put some tees in the bottom, as well.

☞ Monogrammed golf balls and tools for monogramming are available in sports stores or specialty gift catalogs.

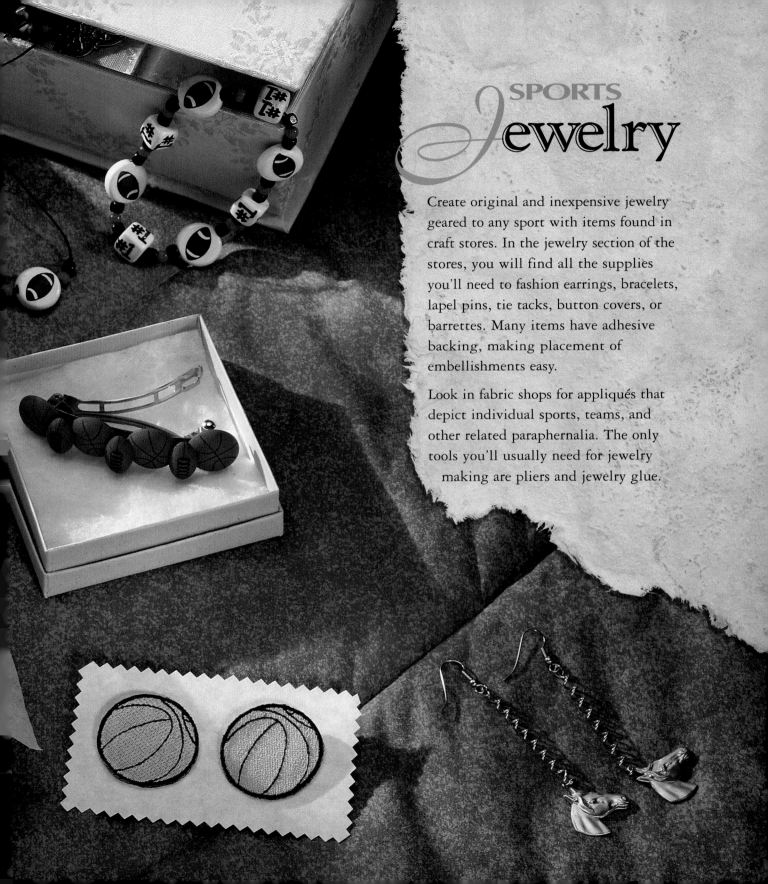

SPORTS
Jewelry

Create original and inexpensive jewelry geared to any sport with items found in craft stores. In the jewelry section of the stores, you will find all the supplies you'll need to fashion earrings, bracelets, lapel pins, tie tacks, button covers, or barrettes. Many items have adhesive backing, making placement of embellishments easy.

Look in fabric shops for appliqués that depict individual sports, teams, and other related paraphernalia. The only tools you'll usually need for jewelry making are pliers and jewelry glue.

Appliqué Earrings

MATERIALS

❖Two posts for pierced or clip-on earrings
❖Jewelry glue or craft glue ❖Two small appliqués in desired design ❖Thin, rigid piece of cardboard, optional

1 Secure appliqués to earring posts, using glue. If appliqué is much larger than the earring post, reinforce it so it will stay rigid. Trim a piece of cardboard the same shape but slightly smaller than the appliqué; then secure the appliqué to the cardboard, using glue.

☞ *Use this technique to secure appliqués to lapel-pin bases, tie-tack bases, or button-cover bases.*

☞ *Give a tie tack with a tie in team colors, or place button covers on a denim shirt*

Dangling charm Earrings

MATERIALS

❖Two crimp necklace ends ❖Two needlenose pliers· ❖Two fishhook earring bases ❖Two metal, glass, or plastic charms

1 Grasp each end of one crimp necklace end with pliers. Pull ends apart gently, stretching the coil.

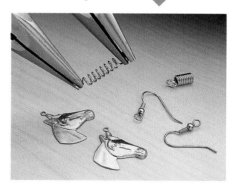

1 Thread the beads onto cording either randomly or in a pattern that alternates sports beads and other beads. If desired, tie a knot between each bead or every third bead. ▶

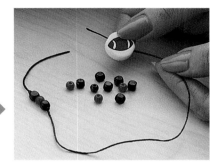

Sports Bracelet

MATERIALS

❖Thin cording or leather strip ❖Beads, with and without a sports theme

2 Continue to thread beads until desired length is achieved; approximately 7" to 8" (18 to 20.5 cm) is necessary to get bracelet over a midsize adult hand. Tie ends of the cording together in a knot. Trim the ends of cording.

☞ *For easier sizing of bracelet, use elastic cording as the base.*

2 Insert end of earring base into loop at end of stretched coil; crimp end with pliers to secure.

3 Attach charm to opposite end of coil, crimping the end with pliers to secure.

☞ *A small number of beads, 5 to 10, depending on their size, can be strung in the middle of a long piece of leather strip or cording for a necklace. Knot the strip at either side of the beads to secure them, if desired. Tie the ends of strip together in a knot.*

SPORTS Wreaths

A decorative wall item like a wreath embellished with sports paraphernalia can be a seasonal or year-round reminder of a person's favorite sport. Wreaths are relatively easy to make and most materials are available at craft stores. Sports-related items and miniatures can be found in craft stores or sports stores.

Embellish a hunting wreath with feathers and stuffed birds, decoys, dried flowers representative of favorite hunting regions, empty shotgun shells, or a photograph of a faithful hunting dog. A wreath for a tennis player could be embellished with miniature tennis racquets, tennis balls, sweat bands, and favorite tennis logos. Use vintage golf clubs, golf balls, tees, and a fantasy score card for a golfer's wreath.

Sports Wreath

MATERIALS

❖Wreath base, made from evergreen, grapevine, or straw ❖Two long embellishments, such as vintage badminton racquets, miniature baseball bats, or small skis ❖22-gauge or 24-gauge paddle floral wire; wire cutter ❖Hot glue gun and glue sticks ❖Additional embellishments, such as badminton birdies, golf balls and tees, tennis balls, baseballs, etc.

1 Place wreath base on flat work surface. Cross long embellishments, such as badminton racquets, so they intersect at the top of the wreath. Secure in place, using floral wire.

2 Secure small or lightweight embellishments randomly on the wreath, using hot glue. Secure large, heavy, or awkward items, using floral wire (opposite).

☞ *With an artificial pine wreath and lightweight embellishments, the flexible wire boughs may be bent around embellishments to secure them, instead of using floral wire.*

Securing large or awkward Embellishments

☞ *Secure heavy or large items, such as frames, decoys, or baseball helmets, to wreath, using floral wire.*

▶

◀

☞ *Some large or awkward items, such as a duck call or miniature baseball bats, may need to have screw eyes inserted into them to aid in wiring onto wreath. Drill pilot holes in item at locations where it can be supported, using a 1/16" drill bit; insert screw eyes in holes.*

Go-to-the-Game
KIT

If you've ever been to a basketball or football game, or watched one on TV, you've probably noticed that the fans really get decked out in their team's colors. Send your sports fan off to the game sufficiently armed for the cheering ahead.

All sorts of clothing, from sweatshirts to caps to earmuffs, are available for purchase. But don't limit yourself to the ready-made items. Use fabric paints to embellish inexpensive canvas tennis shoes or a cap in team colors. Purchase coordinating clothing items, such as a T-shirt and a vest, in solid team colors, and embellish them with pins depicting their team.

In addition to clothes, include face paints or one of the crazy hats you see at games. A simple basketball mask can be made by cutting open a basketball so it will fit over your head, then cutting out two eyeholes. Paint the ball in team colors with acrylic paints, if desired.

Of course, outdoor football games require other necessities, like a stadium blanket, a thermos, hot cocoa mix, hand warmers, and a seat pad. Roll up small items in the blanket, and tie them to the seat pad, using a scarf. If desired, attach game tickets to the bundle.

SNACKS *for the* Armchair quarterbacks

If you're heading over to someone's house to watch the "big game," take along some munchies in a creative container. Souvenir baseball batting hats or football helmets can be used for serving chips, and a miniature hat can be used for dip. Line hats with plastic wrap or a napkin before filling them, if desired.

An inexpensive beach bucket in team colors can be embellished with a team bumper sticker; include the beach shovel for scooping out the snacks. Inflated plastic footballs, basketballs, or soccer balls can be deflated, then cut in half along the molding line, using a utility knife. Touch up cut edges with a permanent-ink marker, if desired. Insert a bowl in one half of the round balls, or place the football half on a kicking tee for stability. A mailing tube can be cut crosswise and painted to create a ring for stabilizing ball bowls.

And what sports event would be complete without chili? On the following pages, you'll find three recipes sure to please a variety of chili lovers. Take the chili to the game party in a slow cooker or large pot, and serve it with bowls of shredded Cheddar cheese, corn chips, and sour cream.

Bill's Prize-Winning Chili

- ❖ 1 lb. (454 g) beef stew meat, cut into 1/2" (1.3 cm) cubes
- ❖ 1 lb. (454 g) hot Italian sausage links, cut into 1/2" (1.3 cm) slices
- ❖ 2 medium onions, coarsely chopped (2 cups/500 mL)
- ❖ 6 cloves garlic, minced
- ❖ 1 can (28 oz./794 g) whole tomatoes, undrained and cut up
- ❖ 1 can (15 oz./425 g) tomato sauce
- ❖ 1/2 cup (125 mL) dry red wine
- ❖ 1/2 cup (125 mL) snipped fresh cilantro
- ❖ 1/4 cup (50 mL) ground ancho chilies*, optional
- ❖ 2 tablespoons (25 mL) sugar
- ❖ 1 tablespoon (15 mL) ground cocoa
- ❖ 1 tablespoon (15 mL) Worcestershire sauce
- ❖ 2 teaspoons (10 mL) dried oregano leaves
- ❖ 1 teaspoon (5 mL) ground cumin
- ❖ Hot pepper sauce
- ❖ 3 cans (16 oz./453 g each) pinto beans, rinsed and drained
- ❖ 1 large green pepper, coarsely chopped (1 1/2 cups/375 mL)

*Ancho chilies are dried poblano chilies. They are about 4" (10 cm) long and are a deep reddish brown, with a mild, rich flavor. They are available in Mexican or specialty markets.

1 Combine beef, sausage, onions, and garlic in 6 to 8-quart (5 3/4 to 7 1/2 L) Dutch oven or stockpot. Cook over medium heat until, beef and sausage are browned and onions are tender-crisp, stirring frequently.

2 Stir in tomatoes, tomato sauce, wine, cilantro, ancho chilies, sugar, cocoa, Worcestershire sauce, oregano, and cumin. Bring to simmer. Reduce heat to low. Simmer for 1 hr., stirring occasionally. Stir in beans and green pepper. Simmer for additional 1/2 hr.

3 Taste chili. Add hot pepper sauce to taste.

Makes 8 to 10 servings

White Chicken Chili

❖ 1 to 2 tablespoons (15 to 30 mL) olive oil
❖ 2 medium onions, chopped (2 cups/500 mL)
❖ 6 cloves garlic, minced
❖ 1 tablespoon (15 mL) ground cumin
❖ 2 teaspoons (10 mL) dried oregano leaves
❖ 1/4 teaspoon (1 mL) ground cloves
❖ 1/4 teaspoon (1 mL) cayenne pepper (or more to taste)
❖ 4 cans (15 1/2 oz./439 g each) Great Northern beans, rinsed and drained
❖ 6 cups (1.5 L) cubed cooked chicken breast*, 1/2" (1.3 cm) cubes
❖ 6 cups (1.5 L) chicken broth
❖ 2 cans (4 oz./113 g each) chopped mild green chilies
❖ 1 cup (250 mL) shredded Monterey Jack cheese

Toppings:
❖ Shredded Monterey Jack cheese
❖ Sour cream
❖ Mild green salsa

*2 lbs. (907 g) fresh chicken breast will yield 6 cups (1.5 L) cubed chicken breast.

1 Heat oil in 6 to 8-quart (6 to 8 L) Dutch oven or stockpot. Add onions and garlic. Cook for 5 to 6 minutes, or until onions are tender, stirring frequently. Stir in cumin, oregano, cloves and cayenne. Cook for 1 minute, stirring frequently.

2 Stir in beans, chicken, broth, and green chilies. Bring to boil over medium-high heat. Reduce heat to low. Simmer for 1 hr., stirring occasionally. Stir in 1 cup (250 mL) cheese until melted. Serve chili with desired toppings.

Makes 8 to 10 servings

Black Bean Chili

❖ 4 cans (15 oz./425 g each) black beans, rinsed and drained, divided
❖ 1 can (14 1/2 oz./411 g each) ready-to-serve vegetable broth
❖ 1 small onion, chopped (1/2 cup/125 mL)
❖ 1 stalk celery, thinly sliced (1/2 cup/125 mL)
❖ 1/3 cup (75 mL) chopped green pepper
❖ 2 cloves garlic, minced
❖ 2 teaspoons (10 mL) olive oil
❖ 1 can (14 1/2 oz./411 g) whole tomatoes, undrained and cut up
❖ 2 teaspoons (10 mL) chili powder
❖ 2 teaspoons (10 mL) ground cumin
❖ 1/2 teaspoon (2 mL) dried oregano leaves
❖ 1/4 teaspoon (1 mL) salt
❖ Chopped seeded tomato
❖ Sliced green onions
❖ Plain nonfat or low-fat yogurt

1 Place 3 cups (750 mL) beans and the broth in food processor or blender. Process until smooth. Set aside.

2 Combine onion, celery, pepper, garlic, and oil in 3-quart (3 L) saucepan. Cook over medium heat for 8 to 10 minutes, or until vegetables are tender, stirring frequently. Stir in processed beans, remaining beans, the canned tomatoes, chili powder, cumin, oregano, and salt.

3 Bring to boil over high heat, stirring occasionally. Reduce heat to low. Simmer for 10 to 15 minutes, or until chili is hot and flavors are blended, stirring occasionally. Garnish each serving with chopped tomato, sliced green onions, and a dollop of yogurt.

Makes 4 to 6 servings

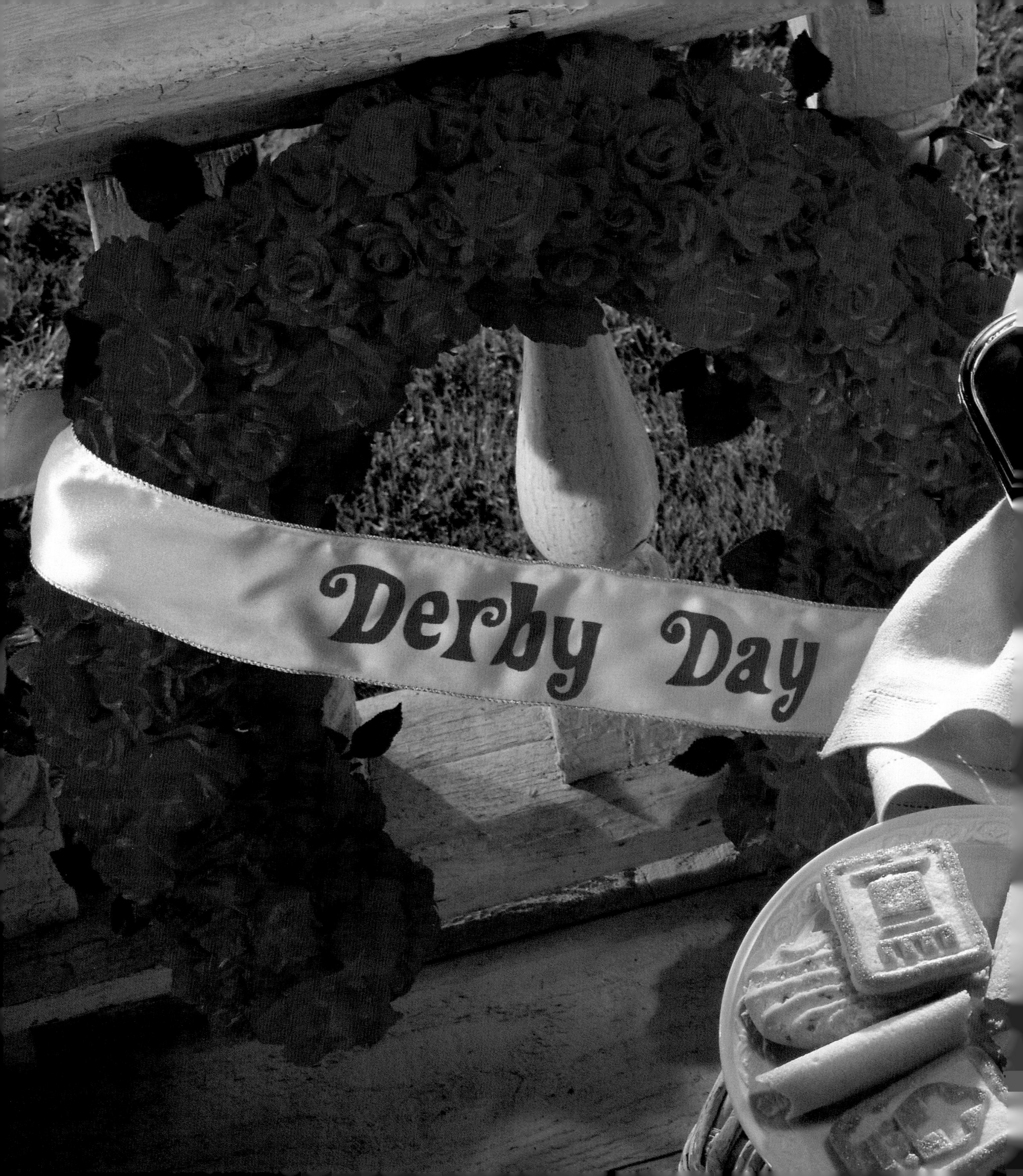
Derby Day

Derby day
KIT

The Kentucky Derby is a tradition-rich event that horse lovers around the country watch faithfully and enjoy. Host a buffet on race day as a gift to your friends and family, or treat your favorite horse lover with some special Derby-related gifts.

Derby Day would not be complete without mint juleps. Follow the recipe on page 89, and serve your juleps in the traditional chilled silver or pewter julep cups. Or create special etched glassware commemorating the event, and present them as a set. Rub-on transfers that resemble etched glass make this an easy project; they are available at craft stores.

A horseshoe-shaped wreath covered with roses completes your Derby festivities. You can easily make one with a foam form and silk roses, available at craft and floral stores.

Run for the roses Wreath

MATERIALS

❖Horseshoe-shaped foam wreath ❖Serrated knife ❖Green paper twist ❖Hot glue gun and glue sticks ❖Silk roses ❖Ribbon in desired color ❖Permanent-ink pen

1 Round off corners and edges of the wreath on one side, using serrated knife. Wrap the wreath completely with paper twist; secure paper twist, using hot glue. Cut rose stems to 1½" (3.8 cm) lengths.

☞ *If horseshoe-shaped wreath is not available, cut one from 2" (5 cm) foam, using serrated knife.*

Etched derby day Glasses

MATERIALS

❖Four tall 8 to 12-oz. (250 to 375 mL) glasses ❖Rub-on transfers for etched glass look, in desired pattern ❖Craft stick or burnishing tool

1 Determine positioning of desired transfers on glassware. If several transfers are on one sheet, cut out the desired transfer.

2 Remove the protective backing from the transfer sheet. Place the transfer exposed-side-down on a glass. Hold transfer firmly in place; rub over the transfer, using craft stick or burnishing tool.

2 Insert rose stems into wreath, placing roses close together. Completely cover top and sides of wreath with roses. Secure roses in place with hot glue, if necessary. ▼

3 Write "Run for the Roses," "Kentucky Derby," or "Derby Day" and the date on the ribbon, using permanent-ink pen. Extend the ribbon diagonally across the wreath; secure ends of ribbon to back of wreath, using hot glue.

Mint Julep

- ❖ 1 tablespoon (15 mL) snipped fresh mint leaves
- ❖ 1 to 2 teaspoons (5 to 10 mL) sugar
- ❖ 1 tablespoon (15 mL) water
- ❖ Finely crushed ice
- ❖ 1 to 2 oz. (30 to 60 g) Kentucky bourbon
- ❖ Fresh mint sprig for garnish

1 Combine mint leaves and sugar in a small bowl or mortar and pestle. Crush mixture with pestle or back of wooden spoon to form a paste. Add water, and stir.

2 Fill a chilled julep cup or tall glass with crushed ice. Add mint syrup and bourbon. Stir well. Garnish with mint sprig.

Makes 1 tall drink

☞ *Cut two straws so they are just longer than the glass is tall, and insert them into crushed ice before serving julep.*

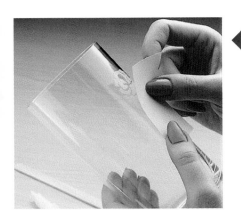

3 Lift transfer sheet slowly, taking care that the entire transfer is released from the sheet. Cover the transfer with the backing sheet; rub over transfer again, to secure it firmly. Repeat with remaining glasses.

☞ *Transfers are available as single motifs, lettering, or graphic motifs.*

☞ *Follow the manufacturer's instructions for specific application of rub-on transfers.*

☞ *Transfers are not permanent, but are durable enough to be washed gently. Some brands are even dishwasher-safe.*

PERSONALIZED
Champagne bottles

Nothing celebrates a momentous occasion or great victory like a bottle of champagne for the winner. From the pop of the cork to the bubbles in the glass, champagne or a sparkling nonalcoholic wine add to the uplifted and euphoric feeling that comes with winning.

Personalize a bottle of bubbly or even a special bottle of wine to commemorate someone's big win. It can be as simple as writing the event, person's name, and date directly on the bottle with a gold paint pen. Or you can create an entire new label for the bottle. Further embellish the bottle with curled ribbon, a photo of the winner, or small medal hung from the neck of the bottle.

Personalized champagne Label

MATERIALS

❖Bottle of champagne ❖Gold art paper
❖Rub-on transfer letters and designs ❖Clear
plastic ruler ❖Aerosol adhesive

1 Measure the size of the existing bottle label. On a piece of scrap paper, draw a copy of the label that is ¼" (6 mm) larger on all sides so it will cover existing label. Cut label shape out of scrap paper.

2 Sketch label design and position of letters and embellishments on scrap paper label. Using scrap paper as template, trace the outline on gold paper. If desired, mark ½" (1.3 cm) intervals along the outside edges of the label to use as a reference guide when positioning transfer letters.

3 Apply rub-on transfer letters to label, following manufacturer's instructions; use clear plastic ruler and reference marks to place letters evenly, and refer to sketch on scrap paper. To center words on label, position the middle letters first, then work outward to the

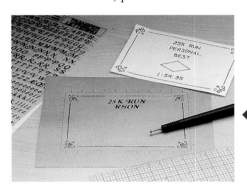

edges. For example, if you are spelling the word "Congratulations," position the letter "u" in the center; then add the "t" and "l" on opposite sides and so on. For words with an even number of letters, position the space between the middle letters in the center.

4 Cut finished label from art paper; cut just inside marked lines. Place label facedown on newspaper-lined work surface. Apply aerosol adhesive to label. Position the new label over label on the bottle, smoothing out any air bubbles; hold in place until adhesive sets.

☞ *Bottle should be at room temperature when securing new label or label may not stay in place.*

INDEX

A

Ankle wallet, 36
Appliqué, fabric-, sweatshirts, 57-59
Appliqué earrings, 74

B

Ball display stands, 5-7
Biking gift ideas, 33, 41-43
Books,
  puzzle scrapbook, 17
  trading card, personalized, 25-27
Bottles, champagne, personalized,
  91-93
Boxes,
  decoupage, 9-11
  shadow, memorabilia, 29-31
Bracelet, 75

C

Camping and hiking gift ideas, 47,
  49, 51
Champagne bottles, personalized,
  91-93
Chili recipes, 84-85
Clock, tee-time, 69-71
Clothing, 53-63
  hat, golf tee, 54-55
  sweatshirts, personalized, 54, 57-59
  T-shirts, remote control, 61-63
Cycling gift ideas, 33, 41-43

D

Dangling charm earrings, 74-75
Decoupage gift ideas, 9-11
Derby Day kit, 87-89
Display stands, balls, 5-7

E

Earrings,
  appliqué, 74
  dangling charm, 74-75
Embellished frame, 20-21
Equipment presentation ideas, 39
Etched Derby Day glasses, 88-89

F

Fabric paint gem accents, 59
Fabric-appliqué sweatshirts, 57-59
Face mask frame, photos, 23
Fishing vests, 47-49
Frames,
  photos, 19-23
  posters, 13-15
  sectionals, 13-15

G

Gem accents, fabric paint, 59
Glass plate, decoupage, 9-11
Glasses, Derby Day, etched, 88-89
Goggles frame, 23
Golf ball frame, 22-23
Golf ball star ornament, 65, 67
Golf lovers gift ideas,
  ball star ornament, 65, 67
  photo frame, 22-23
  tee hat, 54-55
  tee-time clock, 69-71
Golf tee hat, 54-55
Go-to-the-game kit, 81

H

Hat, golf tee, 54-55
Helmets, bike, decorated, 41-43
Hiking and camping gift ideas, 47,
  49, 51
Hinge mounting in shadow boxes, 30
Holiday ornaments, 65-67
Hook and loop mounting in shadow
  boxes, 31
Horse lovers gift ideas, 45, 87-89

I

Ice skate frame, 20-21

J

Jewelry, 73-75

K

Kits,
  Derby Day, 87-89
  go-to-the-game, 81

L

Label, champagne, personalized, 92-93

94

95

CREDITS

CY DECOSSE INCORPORATED

A COWLES MAGAZINES COMPANY

Chairman/CEO: Philip L. Penny
Chairman Emeritus: Cy DeCosse
President/COO: Nino Tarantino
Executive V.P./Editor-in-Chief:
   William B. Jones

GRAND SLAM GIFTS
Created by: The Editors of
   Cy DeCosse Incorporated

Also available from the publisher:
Greet the Season, Toast the Host,
Wrap It Up

Group Executive Editor: Zoe A. Graul
Editorial Manager: Dawn M. Anderson
Senior Editor/Writer: Ellen C. Boeke
Project Manager: Amy Berndt

Associate Creative Director: Lisa Rosenthal
Art Director: Stephanie Michaud
Editor: Janice Cauley
Researchers/Designers: Michael Basler,
   Christine Jahns
Sample Production Manager: Carol Olson
Technical Photo Stylists: Bridget Haugh,
   Sue Jorgensen, Nancy Sundeen
Styling Director: Bobbette Destiche
Project Stylists: Christine Jahns,
   Joanne Wawra
Prop Stylists: Elizabeth Emmons,
   Michele Joy
Food Stylists: Elizabeth Emmons,
   Nancy Johnson
Artisans: Arlene Dohrman,
   Phyllis Galbraith, Valerie Hill,
   Kristi Kuhnau, Virginia Mateen,
   Carol Pilot, Michelle Skudlarek
Vice President of Photography & Production:
   Jim Bindas
Creative Photo Coordinator: Cathleen Shannon
Studio Manager: Marcia Chambers
Lead Photographer: Rebecca Schmitt
Contributing Photographers: Tom Heck,
   Steve Smith

Print Production Manager: Patt Sizer
Desktop Publishing Specialist:
   Laurie Kristensen
Production Staff: Laura Hokkanen,
   Tom Hoops, Jeanette Moss, Mike Schauer,
   Michael Sipe, Brent Thomas, Greg Wallace,
   Kay Wethern
Shop Supervisor: Phil Juntti
Scenic Carpenters: Troy Johnson,
   Rob Johnstone, John Nadeau
Contributors: Chartpack Crafts; Design
   Master; The Fly Angler; Bill Nelson;
   Plaid Enterprises; Richfield High School,
   Athletic Department; Barbara Steele;
   John van Vliet
Printed on American paper by:
   R. R. Donnelley & Sons Co. (0796)

99 98 97 96 / 5 4 3 2 1

Cy DeCosse Incorporated offers
a variety of how-to books. For
information write:
   Cy DeCosse Subscriber Books
   5900 Green Oak Drive
   Minnetonka, MN 55343